ANIMAL SOS!

SAVE THE GORILLA

WINDMILL
BOOKS
New York

Published in 2014 by Windmill Books, An Imprint of Rosen Publishing
29 East 21st Street, New York, NY 10010

Produced for Windmill by Calcium Creative Ltd
Editors for Calcium Creative Ltd: Sarah Eason and Rachel Blount
US Editor: Joshua Shadowens
Designer: Emma DeBanks

Photo credits: Cover: Shutterstock: JKlingebiel. Inside: Dreamstime:
Alangignoux 19, Aughty 12, Mschaap 21, Penumb 12–13, Petegallop 15,
Walleyelj 20, Zaramira 16; Shutterstock: Kitch Bain 22, Beltsazar 28,
Stephane Bidouze 10, Sam Chadwick 1, 24, 26, Pichugin Dmitry 18, FAUP 9,
Eric Gevaert 4, 14, Stephen N Haynes 17, iPics 7, Photodynamic 13,
StockbyMH 6, Pal Teravagimov 25, 27, Trinacria Photo 5, Chris Turner 11,
Sergey Uryadnikov 8, 22–23, Marek Velechovsky 29.

Library of Congress Cataloging-in-Publication Data

Royston, Angela, 1945–
Save the gorilla / by Angela Royston.
pages cm. — (Animal SOS!)
Includes index.
ISBN 978-1-4777-6050-5 (library)— ISBN 978-1-4777-6037-6 (pbk.) —
ISBN 978-1-4777-6052-9 (6-pack)
1. Gorilla—Conservation—Juvenile literature. 2. Endangered species—
Africa—Juvenile literature. I. Title.
QL737.P96R69 2014
599.884—dc23
2013024191

Manufactured in the United States of America
CPSIA Compliance Information: Batch #BW14WM: For Further Information contact Windmill Books, New York, New York at 1-866-478-0556

Contents

Gorillas in Danger

Gorillas are the gentle giants of the forest. These big apes may look fierce, but they usually avoid clashing with other animals. However, gorillas cannot avoid people.

Unequal Conflict

Gorillas are awe-inspiring and magnificent, but people with guns and traps hunt and kill them. Gorillas are a **protected species**, but it is estimated that around 300 are killed illegally every year. There are so few gorillas living in the wild that they are in danger of becoming **extinct**, which means they could die out altogether.

Most gorillas live together in a close family group.

4

Rescue the Gorilla

Gorillas, chimpanzees, and humans all belong to the group of **primates** and are closely related. Most of a gorilla's body is covered in long hair and it has much longer arms than humans. Gorillas can walk on two legs, but they prefer to walk on all fours, using their knuckles. This is called knuckle-walking.

A gorilla's arms are so long its knuckles can easily touch the ground. →

Rescue the GORILLA!

Many people are working hard to save the gorillas, and you can help them. This book will tell you about gorillas and show you what you can do to rescue them.

Gorillas in the wild

Gorillas live only in one area in the world, in a few parts of the rain forest in Central Africa. This is the world's second largest rain forest, after the Amazon rain forest.

Types of Gorillas

There are four different types of gorillas and each type has its own area. Mountain gorillas live in forests high in the mountains on the border between the Democratic Republic of the Congo, Rwanda, and Uganda. Eastern and Western lowland gorillas and Cross River gorillas live in the rain forests and bamboo forests in the **Congo Basin**.

Eastern gorillas are the largest type of gorilla. The males can stand nearly 6 feet (1.8 m) tall.

Gorilla Troops

Although gorillas live in forests, they spend most of their time on the ground. They live together in groups called troops. A troop usually has up to 10 members and is led by an older, strong male. He is in charge of, and looks after, several females and their **offspring**.

ANIMAL SOS!

At one time, scientists thought that Cross River gorillas had already become extinct, but in the 1980s some were seen again in the wild. Today, they are still the rarest type of gorilla.

↑ Some gorilla troops have as many as 30 members, but most are much smaller. This big family of mountain gorillas lives in Rwanda.

Gorillas' Biggest Enemy

Male gorillas are large and heavy. An adult male gorilla is called a silverback and is around twice as heavy as an adult man. Only other gorillas and humans would dare to attack a silverback.

Show of Strength

A silverback protects the females and young gorillas in its troop. Sometimes a younger male challenges the silverback. Then the silverback stands up, beats its chest, and screams. If that does not work, the silverback bares its teeth and charges at the challenger gorilla.

As a male gorilla gets older, the hair on its back becomes gray or silver. That is why it is called a silverback!

Enemy or Friend?

People are the gorillas' greatest enemy. **Poachers** trap and kill gorillas. Farmers and mining companies cut down the gorillas' forests and take over the land. Other people, however, work hard to protect gorillas. They are the gorillas' greatest friends.

Rescue the GORILLA!

Become a friend to the gorillas. Join a **charity** that protects **endangered animals**, such as the World Conservation Society or the World Wildlife Fund. You can have fun raising money to send to the charity.

A gorilla spends much of the day eating leaves and stems of herbs, bushes, and vines.

Losing Their Homes

People are cutting down the gorillas' forests, because they want to mine the gold and precious metals found in the ground. Armies fight each other in the race to find these valuable minerals. The minerals are sold to large international companies, such as cell phone manufacturers.

Caught Up in Wars

Much of the area where gorillas live is not well governed or peaceful. Armies from several countries and **militias** fight for control of land on which gorillas are found. Gorillas and local people are attacked and often lose their homes.

A backhoe knocks down trees and pulls up their roots. It quickly clears a large area of rain forest.

Coltan

The Congo contains large amounts of a dull, black metal called coltan. Coltan is an essential part of cell phones, laptops, and other electronic gadgets. Soldiers clear large areas of the gorillas' forests to reach this precious metal.

In opencast mines all the plants, trees, and soil are removed to reach the gold or other minerals underneath.

Rescue the GORILLA!

Help to save the gorillas' home by telling everyone you know to recycle old cell phones and electronic gadgets. When a cell phone is recycled, the coltan inside it is collected and used again. Reusing coltan means that less coltan is mined.

Logging

Logging is cutting down trees and selling the wood, called timber. The wood of many of the trees in the Congo Basin rain forests is valuable, and so logging is big business there. Logging, however, destroys the gorillas' home.

Scraping a Living

Local people also cut down the trees. The world population is growing fast. The more people there are, the more food and shelter they need. In the Congo Basin, people are moving farther into the forests to cut down valuable timber to sell.

Trucks piled high with tree trunks take newly felled trees to sawmills. Here the trees are cut into planks of timber.

Gorillas Need Forests

Gorillas need forest plants and trees for food and shelter. Each gorilla eats up to 40 pounds (18 kg) of leaves and stems every day. Gorillas also eat fruit, seeds, and roots. However, not all gorillas are totally vegetarian. Lowland gorillas like to eat ants, too.

ANIMAL SOS!

United Nations' scientists have delivered the world a warning. They say that the forests in the Congo Basin are being cut down so fast that the wild gorillas living there could all be extinct by 2025.

Gorillas live peacefully in the rain forest, but how long will the rain forests survive?

Poaching

Killing gorillas is against the law, but that doesn't stop the poachers, people who hunt and kill animals illegally. Poachers kill gorillas because their bodies are valuable. Poachers also sell live gorilla babies as exotic pets.

Making Medicines

Traditional medicines are made from plants, minerals, and parts of dead animals, such as gorillas. Traditional medicines are popular in many countries, but there is no scientific proof that these medicines even work!

Gorilla mothers protect their babies and hold them tight. The baby feels safe when it is close to its mother.

Gorilla Babies

Capturing live baby gorillas as pets is extremely cruel, because the poachers take them from their mothers. Gorilla babies need their mothers. The baby clings to her fur and feeds on her milk. A baby learns to walk at around six months old, but rides on its mother's back for another year.

Older babies ride on their mothers' backs. This leaves the mother free to use her arms and hands.

Rescue the GORILLA!

Raise money to help gorillas by organizing a gorilla party. Send gorilla-shaped invitations and ask people to dress up as gorillas. Decorate cupcakes with chocolate icing in the shape of a gorilla.

Bushmeat

Africans often called forest "the bush," so food from forest animals is called bushmeat. Local people have always eaten some bushmeat, but now wealthy people want it, too.

Trapped

Poachers kill wild animals and sell their meat for high prices in the cities. Poachers often target gorillas because they are so big that each animal provides lots of meat. Sometimes, gorillas are accidentally caught in traps that have been set for other animals.

Young gorillas are very good at climbing trees. This skill helps them to escape from dangers on the ground.

Easy Targets

It is easy for poachers to shoot gorillas, because the animals spend most of their time on the ground, eating. After eating, the gorillas take a nap in a nest made of leaves and branches. Each gorilla builds a new nest every time it sleeps.

Adult males usually nest on the ground, but a female often builds a nest in a tree. A young gorilla shares its mother's nest.

Gorillas in Cameroon are particularly at risk. Workers at mines and logging camps hire their own poachers to supply them with gorilla meat. The roads, which the companies have built through the forest, make it easier for poachers to reach the gorillas.

Human Diseases

Humans kill gorillas by spreading diseases. Gorillas and humans are so similar that they are affected by the same illnesses, which can easily pass from human to gorilla. The **ebola virus** is one of the diseases passed to gorillas.

Deadly Illnesses

The ebola virus causes bleeding inside the body and kills nine out of every ten humans who catch it. It spreads quickly through a group of apes or people. Gorillas catch other human illnesses, too. Many mountain gorillas have died from **pneumonia**.

The ebola virus has swept through many of the areas where gorillas live.

Treating Diseases

A good way to help gorillas is to treat local people. Dr. Kalema-Zikusoka is a vet who treated an outbreak of **scabies** among the mountain gorillas. The disease cleared up only when she treated the local villagers who had the same disease.

Mobile medical units treat villagers who live far away from clinics. Curing the people helps to prevent nearby gorillas from catching the diseases.

ANIMAL SOS!

In the past, gorillas seldom came into contact with humans, but today that has changed. Mountain gorillas are especially at risk. Tourists travel deep into their forests in order to see

Struggling to Survive

Gorillas were safe in the vast Congo Basin rain forests, until people invaded their forests. Now, so few wild gorillas remain, we need to protect them and their forest homes.

A Slow Process

In recent years, the number of gorillas in the wild has decreased alarmingly. Gorillas **breed** slowly so it will take a long time for their numbers to increase. Each female gorilla usually gives birth to just one baby at a time and will probably have less than eight babies altogether.

Every baby gorilla is precious. The mother gorilla does everything she can to help the baby survive.

An Uncertain Life

Many young gorillas die before they reach adulthood. Around half of all gorilla babies die before they are one year old. A young gorilla needs its mother for several years. If poachers kill her, the young gorilla is unlikely to survive.

Young gorillas love to play together. As they grow up, the adults teach them how to survive in the wild.

Rescue the GORILLA!

Collect lots of information, facts, and photos about gorillas. Ask your teacher if you can give a presentation on gorillas, explaining what is happening to them. Try to persuade your class or school to raise money to help the gorillas to survive.

21

Protecting the Forest

The first step to protecting wild gorillas is to protect the forests where they live. Protecting the forests not only helps gorillas but also chimpanzees and all the other animals that live there.

Controlled Logging

Protecting the forest does not mean that all logging must stop. Some trees can be cut down, provided that doing so does not harm the environment. Nature **conservationists** advise logging companies on how to do this scientifically.

There are more than 100,000 Western lowland gorillas, more than any other type of gorilla.

Certified Wood

The Forest Stewardship Council (FSC) is a worldwide organization. If wood has a FSC certificate it means that it has been logged without damaging the forest. The good news is that gorillas and other apes living in FSC forests are doing well. Their numbers are not decreasing.

Western lowland gorillas are doing well because many of them live in protected forests along the Congo River, and the rivers that flow into it.

ANIMAL SOS!

Only 10 to 15 percent of the forests that grow on both sides of the Congo River are FSC protected. This means that gorillas and other animals in the remaining 85 to 90 percent are still in grave danger.

Protecting the Gorillas

Many different charities and other organizations are working hard to protect the gorillas. One of the best ways to save wildlife is to set up a national park or nature reserve.

National Parks

A national park is an area of land that is protected by law. People are forbidden from doing anything, such as farming or mining, that would harm the environment. National parks help the local people, because they bring tourists into the area.

Around 300 mountain gorillas live in the Volcanoes National Park in Rwanda. They share the park with elephants, monkeys, and other animals.

Guarding the Parks

Setting up a national park alone is not enough to protect the gorillas and other animals from poachers. **Park rangers** with guns patrol the parks. They look for animal traps set by poachers and for signs that animals have been killed by poachers.

Park rangers use long sticks to find animal traps. They carry guns in case they are attacked. Their boots and clothes protect them from snakes and insects.

ANIMAL SOS!

Virunga National Park was Africa's first national park. At least 200 mountain gorillas live there and thousands of local people use it for fishing. The park is now threatened, because the Congolese government may allow oil companies into the park to drill for oil.

Tourism

Gorilla treks to see the gorillas in their natural homes is big business. Tourism helps the local people and the gorillas, provided it is well managed. Tourists must respect the gorillas!

Keep Your Distance

Gorillas are shy and easily disturbed. Scientists have found that if people come too close, the gorillas stop eating and the males become angry. They advise that tourists and scientists should try to keep 20 yards (18 m) away from gorillas.

Tourists visit national parks to see gorillas, especially baby gorillas. There are also many other beautiful animals and birds to see.

Park Rules

National parks have rules to protect the gorillas. Only a small group of tourists can look for gorillas at a time. Each group is led by guards, who protect the tourists from the animals.

Rescue the GORILLA!

Find out about gorillas by visiting a zoo. Ask your teacher if the school can organize a class visit to a local zoo that has gorillas. Mountain gorillas do not survive well in zoos, so the gorillas you see will be lowland gorillas.

Tourists often have to trek for miles (km) through difficult countryside before they see a gorilla.

Will Wild Gorillas Survive?

Only a few wild gorillas remain in just one part of Africa. The forests where they live are getting smaller, and they have nowhere else to go. Will these magnificent animals soon survive only in zoos?

Hazardous Future

Gorillas have many things working against them. People are taking over their forests, they are dying from human diseases, and poachers are killing them. There is hope, but urgent action is needed.

It is easy to see gorillas in a zoo. This is fun for people, but it is unnatural for the gorillas.

Taking Action

Charities, international organizations, and governments need to act quickly. More national parks are needed. All the forests in the Congo Basin need to be FSC protected. Governments in the area must not allow oil, gas, or mining companies to operate in their national parks.

Scientists study gorillas in zoos. The more they understand about gorillas, the more they can help them to survive.

Rescue the GORILLA!

Tell your family and friends not to buy **hardwood** that has been logged from the rain forests, unless it has a FSC certificate. Tell them to buy reclaimed wood instead. This is wood that has been used before.

breed (BREED) To produce young.

charity (CHER-uh-tee) An organization that raises money, and runs projects, to help those who need it.

Congo Basin (KON-goh BAY-sin) The area of land from which water flows into the River Congo or its tributaries.

conservationists (kon-ser-VAY-shun-ists) People who work to protect the environment.

ebola virus (ih-BOH-lah VY-rus) A deadly virus that causes a high temperature and bleeding inside the body.

endangered animals (in-DAYN-jerd A-nuh-mulz) Animals, such as gorillas, which are in danger of becoming extinct.

extinct (ik-STINGKT) No longer existing.

hardwood (HARD-wood) Wood from trees, such as oak, mahogany, and teak, which are not conifer trees.

militias (muh-LIH-shuhz) An army or group of soldiers, who may not be controlled by the government.

offspring (OF-spring) An animal's baby or young.

park rangers (PARK RAYN-jerz) People employed by a national park or nature reserve to guard and protect its wildlife.

pneumonia (noo-MOH-nyuh) A disease that affects the lungs.

poachers (POH-churz) People who kill wild animals illegally, usually for food or to sell parts of the animals' bodies.

primates (PRY-mayts) The group of animals that includes monkeys, apes, and humans.

protected species (pruh-TEKT-ed SPEE-sheez) A type of living thing that is protected by law from being harmed.

scabies (SKAY-beez) A skin disease caused by mites.

Further Reading

Clark, Willow. Gorillas: *Life in the Troop.* Animal Families. New York: PowerKids Press, 2011.

Nichols, Michael and Elizabeth Carney. *Face to Face with Gorillas.* Face to Face with Animals. Des Moines, IA: National Geographic Children's Books, 2009.

Portman, Michael. *Gorillas in Danger.* Animals at Risk. New York: Gareth Stevens Learning Library, 2011.

Simon, Seymour. *Gorillas.* New York: Harper Collins, 2008.

Websites

For web resources related to the subject of this book, go to: www.windmillbooks.com/weblinks and select this book's title.

Index